Disney PRINCESS

Royal Recipe

COLLECTION

Meredith₀ Books
Des Moines, Iowa

Meredith Books
1716 Locust Street
Des Moines, IA 50309–3023
meredithbooks.com

Printed in China.

First Edition.
ISBN: 978-0-696-24118-5

Writer/Editor: Stephanie Karpinske, M.S., R.D.
Art Direction: Chad Jewell

Contents

Hi, I'm Pocahontas. Welcome to
The Royal Recipe Collection. This book
is full of recipes fit for a princess, her
friends, and family. So check out
these chapters and get ready to cook!

The Royal Cooking Academy Recipe Basics

Every princess needs to know so many important things, such as how to make snacks and meals. This cookbook will help you with that, but before you begin cooking, read these cooking tips that Mulan learned at the prestigious Royal Cooking Academy.

BEFORE YOU BEGIN

- Read the entire recipe from beginning to end with an adult. Ask yourself: Do I know exactly what I'm supposed to do? If there's anything you don't understand, ask the adult for help.
- If you have any food allergies, read the ingredients carefully to be sure all the foods are safe for you to eat.
- Check your ingredients. Make sure you have enough of all the required ingredients. If you don't, make a list of the things you need, and ask an adult to help you get them.
- Check your utensils. Gather all the utensils and equipment you'll need to complete the recipe. If you're missing anything, ask an adult for help.
- Always wash your hands with soap and water for at least 20 seconds before you start cooking.

PREPARING INGREDIENTS

- Wash fresh fruits and veggies in cool water before preparing or eating them.
- Use only clean, uncracked eggs.

WHEN MAKING THE RECIPE

- Measure ingredients accurately.
- Follow each recipe step by step. Finish each step in the recipe before starting the next. Don't take shortcuts!
- Use good food-safety habits. Cook and eat only fresh foods. After working with eggs, raw poultry, seafood, or meat, wash your hands, equipment, and any work surfaces, including cutting boards and countertops.
- Be safe. Children should not use knives or other sharp equipment without an adult's permission and supervision.

WHEN YOU'RE DONE

- Put away leftovers as soon as possible. Never let food sit out for more than two hours.
- Put away all ingredients and equipment.
- Clean up. Throw away trash, such as food wrappers and empty packages. Load dirty dishes in the dishwasher or wash, dry, and put them away. Wipe the counters and table with hot, soapy water.

When the Clock Strikes Breakfast

Wake up, little princess! It's time for breakfast (or "Breefus," as Gus would say). And with all of these recipes to pick from, you can choose a different breakfast every day.

Egg Casserole

Ingredients

Shortening

6 slices whole wheat bread or 4 whole wheat English muffins, halved

1 cup reduced-fat shredded cheddar cheese

6 eggs

2 cups low-fat milk

2 teaspoons yellow mustard

¼ teaspoon salt

⅛ teaspoon black pepper

Utensils

2-quart rectangular baking dish

Measuring cups

4-cup measuring cup or medium bowl

Measuring spoons

Rotary beater or fork

Plastic wrap

Hot pads

Wire cooling rack

1. Grease the baking dish with shortening. Tear bread or English muffin halves into bite-size pieces. Sprinkle half of the bread pieces into the bottom of the baking dish.

2. Sprinkle cheese over bread pieces in baking dish. Sprinkle remaining bread pieces over cheese.

3. Crack eggs into a 4-cup measuring cup or medium bowl. Add milk, mustard, salt, and pepper to eggs. Mix with the rotary beater or fork until all ingredients are well blended. Pour egg mixture over bread layers in the baking dish. Cover dish with plastic wrap.

4. Chill in the refrigerator for at least 2 hours, but not more than 24 hours.

5. Preheat the oven to 325°F. Remove plastic wrap from baking dish. Put dish in the oven. Bake for 40 to 45 minutes or until edges are puffed and the center is set.

6. Use hot pads to remove baking dish from oven. Turn off oven. Place baking dish on the cooling rack for 10 minutes. Cut into squares to serve. Makes 6 servings.

Nutrition Facts per serving: 194 calories, 9 g total fat, 219 mg cholesterol, 279 mg sodium, 14 g carbohydrate, 2 g fiber, 14 g protein.

Princess Party Tips

Serve this egg casserole alongside a platter of fruit. Fill the platter with grapes, orange slices, strawberries, or any of your favorite fruits.

This casserole can be made and then refrigerated overnight so when morning comes you just pop it in the oven. It's perfect for the day of the royal ball, when everyone needs plenty of time to get ready.

Triangles
Fit for a Mouse

Ingredients

¾ cup reduced-fat shredded cheddar cheese (3 ounces)

4 7- to 8-inch whole wheat or plain flour tortillas

3 ounces thinly sliced cooked ham

⅔ cup chopped tomato

Bottled salsa (optional)

Utensils

Measuring cups
Large skillet
Wide metal spatula
Cutting board
Hot pads
Sharp knife

1 Sprinkle cheese over half of each tortilla. Top with ham and tomato. Fold tortillas in half to form quesadillas, pressing together gently.

2 Place two of the quesadillas in the skillet. Place the skillet on the stove burner. Turn the burner to medium heat.

3 Cook tortillas for $1\frac{1}{2}$ to 2 minutes or until cheese begins to melt. Use the wide metal spatula to flip the quesadillas over. Cook $1\frac{1}{2}$ to 2 minutes more or until golden brown. Use the wide metal spatula to move quesadillas to the cutting board. Repeat with the remaining two quesadillas. Turn off the burner. Use the hot pads to remove the skillet from the burner. Place hot skillet on another hot pad to cool.

4 Use the sharp knife to cut each quesadilla into wedges. If you like, serve with salsa. Makes 4 servings.

Nutrition Facts per serving: 230 calories, 9 g total fat, 24 mg cholesterol, 753 mg sodium, 17 g carbohydrate, 11 g fiber, 18 g protein.

As a mouse, Jaq and his sidekick, Gus, love anything made with cheese. If you do too, try these cheese-filled quesadillas.

Fairy Godmother Wands

Ingredients

Nonstick cooking spray

1 egg

⅓ cup low-fat milk

¼ teaspoon vanilla

Dash ground cinnamon

4 thick slices of bread (such as Texas-style toast bread)

½ cup orange juice

1 tablespoon honey

1 teaspoon cornstarch

⅛ teaspoon ground cinnamon

1 tablespoon powdered sugar

Utensils

Large baking sheet

Foil

Pie plate

Rotary beater or fork

Measuring cups

Measuring spoons

Wide metal spatula

Hot pads

Small saucepan

Wooden spoon

1 Preheat the oven to 450°F. Line the baking sheet with foil; coat foil with cooking spray. Save until Step 2. Crack egg into the pie plate. Beat with the rotary beater or fork until yolk and white are mixed together. Add milk, vanilla, and a dash of cinnamon. Beat until ingredients are well mixed.

2 Dip one slice of bread into egg mixture. Turn over bread with a wide metal spatula to coat the other side. Put coated bread on the baking sheet. Repeat with remaining bread slices.

3 Put baking sheet in oven. Bake about 8 minutes or until bread is lightly browned. Use hot pads to remove pan from oven. Carefully turn bread slices over using the wide metal spatula. Use hot pads to return pan to oven. Bake for 5 to 8 minutes more or until golden brown.

4 While French toast is baking, make the orange syrup. Put the orange juice, honey, cornstarch, and ⅛ teaspoon cinnamon in the saucepan. Put saucepan on the burner. Turn the burner to medium heat. Cook and stir with the wooden spoon until mixture is thickened and bubbly. Turn burner to low heat. Cook and stir for 2 minutes more. Turn off burner. Use hot pads to remove saucepan from burner, placing hot saucepan on another hot pad to cool.

5 Cut each piece of toast into three or four sticks to resemble wands. Sprinkle toast wands with powdered sugar and served with orange syrup. Makes 4 servings.

Nutrition Facts per serving: 187 calories, 5 g total fat, 104 mg cholesterol, 267 mg sodium, 31 g carbohydrate, 0 g fiber, 9 g protein.

Princess Party Tips

Put the orange syrup in pretty little teacups for your guests to dunk their wands in.

This French toast is cut into sticks that look like little fairy wands. Dust on a little powdered sugar to make them sparkle.

Pumpkin Carriage Waffles

Ingredients

Nonstick cooking spray

2 cups all-purpose flour

2 tablespoons packed brown sugar

1 tablespoon baking powder

½ teaspoon salt

½ teaspoon pumpkin pie spice

2 eggs

1½ cups low-fat milk

1 cup canned pumpkin

2 tablespoons cooking oil

Orange wedges (optional)

Utensils

Electric waffle baker

Measuring cups

Measuring spoons

2 medium mixing bowls

Wooden spoon

2 forks

Hot pad

Serving plate

Foil

1 Lightly spray waffle baker grids with cooking spray before preheating waffle baker.

2 Put flour, brown sugar, baking powder, salt, and pumpkin pie spice in a mixing bowl. Stir with the wooden spoon to mix. Save until Step 4.

3 Crack the eggs into the other mixing bowl. Beat with a fork until yolks and whites are mixed together. Add milk, canned pumpkin, and cooking oil to eggs. Beat with the fork until ingredients are well mixed.

4 Add the egg mixture to the flour mixture. Stir with the wooden spoon until dry ingredients are wet.

5 Pour about ¾ cup waffle batter onto grids of preheated waffle baker. Close lid quickly; do not open until done.* When done, use a hot pad to lift lid and use other fork to lift waffle off grid. Place on a serving plate. Cover with foil to keep warm. Repeat until all the batter is used. Turn off waffle baker. If you like, serve with orange wedges. Makes 10 servings.

Nutrition Facts per serving: 164 calories, 4 g total fat, 44 mg cholesterol, 221 mg sodium, 26 g carbohydrate, 1 g fiber, 5 g protein.

*Note: All waffle bakers are different. For timing on how long to cook your waffle, check the directions that came with your waffle baker.

A little magic
turns a pumpkin
into a carriage for
Cinderella, but here,
pumpkin adds a
little magic to
your waffles.

Stepsister Circle-wiches

Ingredients

8   slices whole wheat bread

¼   cup peanut butter

¼   cup raisins

1   cup sliced or chopped bananas

Utensils

4-inch round cookie cutter or desired shape cookie cutter

Table knife

Small spoon

Measuring cups

Plastic wrap, if using

1 Use the cookie cutter to cut each bread slice into circles. Use the knife to spread peanut butter on 4 of the bread circles. Use the spoon to divide the raisins and bananas on top of the peanut butter. Top with remaining bread rounds. Serve the sandwiches immediately or wrap in plastic wrap and chill in the refrigerator for up to 2 hours. Makes 4 servings.

Nutrition Facts per serving: 278 calories, 10 g total fat , 0 mg cholesterol, 311 mg sodium, 40 g carbohydrate, 6 g fiber, 11 g protein.

Princess Party Tips

Let your guests help make these sandwiches. Set out different cookie cutters and let your friends pick which one they want to use.

Anastasia likes to create extra work for Cinderella, such as having her cut the crusts off a sandwich. When you make this crustless sandwich at home, you can cut it into any fun shape using a cookie cutter.

Picky Eaters' Fruit Sundae

Ingredients

1   cup fresh blueberries, grapes, strawberries, and/or 2 small bananas, peeled

1   6-ounce carton vanilla low-fat yogurt

½   to 1 cup ready-to-eat unsweetened cereal such as bran cereal flakes, round toasted oat cereal, and/or oat square cereal

Utensils

Cutting board
Sharp knife
Measuring cups
Small spoon
2 serving bowls

1   If using strawberries, put them on the cutting board and use the sharp knife to cut off the green tops. Cut the strawberries into bite-size pieces. If using bananas, put them on the cutting board and use the knife to cut them into bite-size pieces.

2   Divide yogurt in half and spoon each half into a serving bowl. Divide cereal and fruit in half and put into bowls with yogurt. Serve right away. Makes 2 servings.

Nutrition Facts per serving: 149 calories, 2 g total fat, 4 mg cholesterol, 126 mg sodium, 31 g carbohydrate, 3 g fiber, 6 g protein.

Drizella is hard to please, but this sundae lets her choose whichever fruit she wants so she's sure to like it.

The Prince's Royal Mix

Ingredients

4 cups multigrain cereal with rolled rye, oats, barley, and wheat

1 cup regular rolled oats

¾ cup coarsely chopped almonds or pecans, toasted

1 6-ounce package dried cranberries

½ cup dried banana chips, coarsely crushed

Vanilla low-fat yogurt or low-fat milk (optional)

Utensils

Measuring cups

Large mixing bowl

Large spoon

Large tightly covered container

1 Put the cereal, rolled oats, almonds, cranberries, and crushed banana chips in the large bowl. Stir with the spoon to mix.

2 Put the cereal mix in the container. Cover tightly. Store in the refrigerator up to 4 weeks. If you like, serve with yogurt or milk. Makes about 7 cups (fourteen ½-cup servings).

Nutrition Facts per serving: 157 calories, 5 g total fat, 0 mg cholesterol, 60 mg sodium, 27 g carbohydrate, 4 g fiber, 4 g protein.

Royalty, like Prince Charming, won't eat just any cereal. They like to make their own royal mix, just like this one. Eat it with milk, yogurt, or on its own.

Princess Party Tips

Serve this cereal mix in a pretty teacup and your guests will feel like royalty.

Get Your Work Done Smoothies

Ingredients

2   ripe bananas

1   cup frozen unsweetened whole strawberries

1   6-ounce carton vanilla low-fat yogurt

¾ cup low-fat milk

Fresh whole strawberries (optional)

Utensils

Cutting board
Table knife
Measuring cups
Electric blender
3 serving glasses
Rubber scraper

1 Remove the peel from the bananas and throw away. Place the bananas on the cutting board. Use the knife to cut bananas into chunks.

2 Put banana chunks, frozen strawberries, yogurt, and milk in the blender.

3 Cover the blender with the lid and blend on high speed until the fruit mixture is smooth. Turn off the blender. Pour mixture into the serving glasses. Use the rubber scraper to get all of the drink out of the blender. If you like, top the drinks with whole strawberries. Makes 3 (about 8-ounce) servings.

Nutrition Facts per serving: 159 calories, 2 g total fat, 6 mg cholesterol, 66 mg sodium, 33 g carbohydrate, 3 g fiber, 6 g protein.

Cinderella's stepmother gives her so many chores that sometimes she only has time for a quick breakfast, like this smoothie. If your mornings are busy too, try this fruit-filled drink.

Whistle While You Lunch

When the Dwarfs head off to work, they need to take a hearty lunch. You need a good lunch too. Try one of these recipes and you'll soon be whistling a happy tune.

Don't Be So Grumpy Cups

Ingredients

½ cup light mayonnaise

½ teaspoon dried dillweed or lemon-pepper seasoning

1 9-ounce package refrigerated cooked chicken breast strips, coarsely chopped

¾ cup chopped broccoli

¼ cup shredded carrots

Whole grain crackers (optional)

Utensils

Measuring cups
Measuring spoons
Small bowl
Wooden spoon
Medium bowl

1 Put mayonnaise and dillweed in the small bowl. Stir with the wooden spoon to mix.

2 Put chicken, broccoli, and carrots in the medium bowl. Pour mayonnaise mixture over chicken mixture; toss to coat. Cover and refrigerate for up to 24 hours. If you like, serve with crackers. Makes 4 servings.

Nutrition Facts per serving: 174 calories, 11 g total fat, 44 mg cholesterol, 401 mg sodium, 4 g carbohydrate, 1 g fiber, 16 g protein.

When you're having a rough morning, chill out at lunchtime with this cold chicken salad served in a cup. It always cheers up Grumpy (well, at least a little …).

Trick-Free Tuna

Ingredients

1   3-ounce can chunk white tuna (water pack), drained and flaked

½   cup packaged shredded cabbage with carrot (coleslaw mix)

2   tablespoons plain low-fat yogurt

2   tablespoons bottled reduced-fat Ranch salad dressing

2   whole grain rolls, split

Utensils
Small bowl
Measuring cups
Measuring spoons
Wooden spoon
Plastic wrap

1 Put tuna in the bowl. Add coleslaw mix, yogurt, and salad dressing; mix well with wooden spoon. Serve at once or cover bowl with plastic wrap and refrigerate for as long as 4 hours before serving.

2 Evenly divide the tuna mixture between the roll bottoms. Cover with roll tops. Makes 2 servings.

Nutrition Facts per serving: 217 calories, 6 g total fat, 23 mg cholesterol, 535 mg sodium, 25 g carbohydrate, 3 g fiber, 15 g protein.

The witch transformed herself into an ugly old crone to trick Snow White into eating the poison apple. But there's no tricks needed for this Ranch-flavored tuna—everyone will want a bite.

No Need to Sneeze Sandwiches

Ingredients

Nonstick cooking spray

4 slices whole wheat bread

2 tablespoons bottled barbecue sauce

2 slices reduced-fat process American cheese

2 ounces thinly sliced smoked turkey

Utensils

Table knife
Measuring spoons
Medium skillet
Wide metal spatula
Hot pads
Wire cooling rack
Kitchen scissors

1 Lightly coat one side of each bread slice with cooking spray. Use the table knife to spread barbecue sauce on the plain side of two of the bread slices. Add a slice of cheese and smoked turkey to both bread slices. Top with remaining bread slices, plain sides down. Place sandwiches on the skillet.

2 Put skillet on a stove burner. Turn the burner to medium heat. Cook sandwiches about 3 minutes or until bottom slices of bread are toasted and cheese begins to melt. Use the wide metal spatula to turn sandwiches over. Cook for 1 to 2 minutes more or until bottom slice of bread is toasted and cheese is melted. Turn off burner. Use hot pads to remove skillet from burner to cooling rack. Use the wide metal spatula to remove sandwich from skillet. Use scissors to cut sandwiches into triangles. Serve immediately. Makes 2 sandwiches.

Nutrition Facts per sandwich: 260 calories, 8 g total fat, 31 mg cholesterol, 1,172 mg sodium, 30 g carbohydrate, 4 g fiber, 16 g protein.

Princess Party Tips

Serve these triangle-shaped sandwiches piled high on a pretty cake stand.

These grilled cheese sandwiches, made with turkey and barbecue sauce, are nothing to sneeze at—well, unless you're Sneezy, that is.

aaahCHOO!

Not Too Messy
Roll-ups

Ingredients

1   small banana, peeled

⅓   cup peanut butter

4   7- to 8-inch whole
    wheat or white flour
    tortillas

1   cup chopped
    strawberries

¼   cup low-fat granola

Utensils
Medium bowl
Fork
Measuring cups
Wooden spoon
Table knife
Sharp knife

1 Put the banana in the bowl. Mash with the fork. Add the peanut butter to the mashed banana. Stir with the wooden spoon to mix.

2 Use the table knife to spread peanut butter mixture over tortillas. Sprinkle with strawberries and granola. Tightly roll up tortillas. Use the sharp knife to cut each roll-up into 1-inch pieces. Serve immediately or wrap pieces in plastic wrap and refrigerate for up to 4 hours. Makes 4 servings.

Nutrition Facts per serving: 308 calories, 15 g total fat, 0 mg cholesterol, 433 mg sodium, 31 g carbohydrate, 13 g fiber, 14 g protein.

Snow White is constantly picking up after those messy Dwarfs, but this sandwich holds everything together in a tortilla so the Dwarfs make less of a mess. If you're a little messy too, give it a try!

Walk in the Woods Salad

Ingredients

- ¼ cup orange juice
- 1 tablespoon salad oil
- 2 teaspoons honey mustard or Dijon-style mustard
- 1 teaspoon sugar
- ¼ teaspoon salt
- 4 cups torn mixed lettuce
- 12 ounces cooked, boneless turkey breast, cut into bite-size chunks
- 1½ cups fresh blueberries, raspberries, or quartered strawberries
- 2 tablespoons bite-size fish-shape whole grain crackers

Utensils
Measuring cups
Measuring spoons
Screw-top jar with lid
Medium bowl
Tongs
4 salad plates

1 To make the dressing, put the orange juice, oil, mustard, sugar, and salt in the screw-top jar. Tightly cover with the lid. Shake until combined. Put the lettuce in the medium bowl. Drizzle the dressing over the lettuce. Using the tongs, gently toss the lettuce to coat with the dressing. Divide the lettuce among the salad plates.

2 Put the turkey and fruit on the lettuce. Sprinkle with the crackers. Makes 4 main-dish servings.

Nutrition Facts per serving: 205 calories, 5 g total fat, 71 mg cholesterol, 240 mg sodium, 12 g carbohydrate, 3 g fiber, 27 g protein.

Princess Party Tips
Set out bowls of blueberries, raspberries, and strawberries and your friends can choose which type of berries they want in their salad.

Snow White often gathers berries from the woods, but you can get them at the store for this berry fresh salad. The fish-shape crackers make this salad extra fun!

Wishing Well Pasta

Ingredients

- 4 ounces dried multigrain rotini (1½ cups)
- 4 ounces cooked lean ham, cut into bite-size pieces
- 1 cup snow peas or sugar snap peas, trimmed
- ½ cup bottled reduced-calorie Ranch salad dressing
- ¾ cup grape or cherry tomatoes, halved

Utensils

Measuring cups
Large saucepan
Hot pads
Colander
Wooden spoon
Large bowl
Plastic wrap

1 Cook rotini pasta in the large saucepan following the pasta package directions. Turn off the burner. Use hot pads to remove saucepan from burner. Place colander in sink. Carefully pour pasta into the colander to drain. Run cold water over the pasta in colander. Stir pasta with wooden spoon. Run cold water over pasta again.

2 Put drained pasta, ham, and peas in the large bowl. Stir with wooden spoon until combined. Pour dressing over pasta mixture. Stir gently with wooden spoon until pasta is coated. Cover with plastic wrap. Refrigerate for at least 2 hours or up to 24 hours.

3 To serve, add tomatoes to pasta and ham mixture. Stir gently with a clean wooden spoon. Makes 4 main-dish servings.

Nutrition Facts per serving: 236 calories, 10 g total fat, 25 mg cholesterol, 687 mg sodium, 26 g carbohydrate, 3 g fiber, 11 g protein.

Tip: Ask an adult to help you cook the pasta in the boiling water and drain it in the colander.

Serve this salad in a deep bowl so it looks like a wishing well. Then take a bite and make a wish. If you make lots of wishes, one is bound to come true!

I'm *Soooo* Sleepy Soup

Ingredients

2 14-ounce cans reduced-sodium chicken broth

2 cups water

¼ teaspoon black pepper

1 cup dried multigrain elbow macaroni

1½ cups thinly sliced carrots

1½ cups frozen whole kernel corn

1½ cups cubed cooked chicken (about 8 ounces)

¼ cup finely shredded Parmesan cheese

Crisp wheat breadsticks (optional)

Utensils

Measuring cups
Measuring spoons
Large saucepan with lid
Wooden spoon
Hot pads
Wire cooling rack
Soup ladle
6 soup bowls

1 Put chicken broth, water, and pepper in the saucepan. Put the saucepan on a stove burner. Turn the burner to high heat. Heat until broth mixture begins to boil. Add macaroni and turn the burner to medium-high heat. Cover saucepan with lid and cook for 5 minutes. Stir macaroni mixture often with the wooden spoon. Use hot pads to remove lid. Turn the burner to medium heat. Stir in carrots and corn. Return to boiling, then turn the burner to medium-low heat. Cover and cook for 5 to 8 minutes more or until vegetables and pasta are tender. Stir in the chicken. Turn off burner. Use hot pads to remove saucepan from burner to cooling rack.

2 Use a soup ladle to evenly divide the soup into bowls. Sprinkle each serving with cheese. If you like, serve with breadsticks. Makes 6 servings.

Nutrition Facts per serving: 200 calories, 4 g total fat, 35 mg cholesterol, 426 mg sodium, 23 g carbohydrate, 3 g fiber, 18 g protein.

Princess Party Tips

Make this soup for your next slumber party. It might make you sleepy so make sure your sleeping bags are ready!

Sleepy has a hard-enough time staying
awake, and this warm, yummy soup makes
him even sleepier. Try it on a cold, windy day
and you too may want to take a little nap.

Magic Mirror Soup

Ingredients

2 14-ounce cans reduced-sodium chicken broth

2 cups frozen loose-pack pepper stir-fry vegetables (yellow, green, and red sweet peppers, and onions)

1 14½-ounce can diced tomatoes, undrained

2 cups chopped cooked chicken

1 cup crushed packaged baked tortilla chips (about 2 cups uncrushed)

Shredded reduced-fat cheddar cheese and/or chopped avocado (optional)

Utensils
Measuring cups
Large saucepan
Wooden spoon
Hot pads
Wire cooling rack
Soup ladle
4 soup bowls

1 Put chicken broth, vegetables, undrained tomatoes, and chicken in the saucepan. Put the saucepan on a stove burner. Turn the burner to high heat. Heat until soup begins to boil. Turn burner to medium heat. Cover and cook for 3 to 5 minutes or until vegetables are tender. Stir soup occasionally with the wooden spoon. Turn off burner. Use hot pads to remove saucepan from burner to a cooling rack.

2 Ladle soup into bowls and sprinkle with crushed tortilla chips. If desired, top with cheese and/or chopped avocado. Makes 4 servings.

Nutrition Facts per serving: 233 calories, 6 g total fat, 62 mg cholesterol, 842 mg sodium, 20 g carbohydrate, 4 g fiber, 26 g protein.

What's the fairest soup in the land? This one! Top it with tortilla chips, cheese, or even chopped avocado.

Ariel learns that being a princess means hosting tea parties. But what will she serve? These mini cucumber sandwiches, of course.

Speechless Sweet Fries

Ingredients

2 medium sweet potatoes (about 1 pound)
2 tablespoons cooking oil
¼ teaspoon salt
⅛ teaspoon black pepper
⅓ cup light dairy sour cream
1 tablespoon orange juice

Utensils

Vegetable brush
Vegetable peeler
Sharp knife
Large plastic bag
Measuring spoons
15x10x1-inch baking pan
Hot pads
Wire cooling rack
Measuring cups
Small bowl
Small spoon

1 Preheat the oven to 450°F. Scrub sweet potatoes with vegetable brush. If desired, use vegetable peeler to remove peel from potatoes. Cut potatoes into ¼-inch-thick wedges with the sharp knife. Put potato wedges in plastic bag.

2 Put oil, salt, and pepper in the bag with the potatoes. Seal plastic bag. Shake well to coat potatoes with oil mixture.

3 Put potatoes in a single layer on the baking pan. Place baking pan in oven. Bake about 25 minutes or until potatoes are lightly browned and tender. Turn off oven. Use hot pads to remove pan from oven and place on cooling rack.

4 Put the sour cream and orange juice in the bowl. Stir with a spoon until combined. Serve fries with sour cream mixture. Makes 6 servings.

Nutrition Facts per serving: 93 calories, 6 g total fat, 4 mg cholesterol, 128 mg sodium, 10 g carbohydrate, 1 g fiber, 1 g protein.

Ariel lost her voice when she got her legs. You'll be speechless too after you taste these sweet potato fries. They're that good!

Dinglehopper Dips

Ingredients

1   4-ounce container vanilla pudding

½   teaspoon vanilla

¼   teaspoon ground cinnamon

¼   of an 8-ounce container frozen light whipped dessert topping, thawed

¾   cup low-fat granola

3   cups assorted fresh fruit such as sliced apples, banana chunks, or strawberries

Utensils

Measuring spoons
Medium bowl
Small spoon
Rubber scraper
2 small serving bowls
Fork

1   For the dip, put pudding, vanilla, and ground cinnamon in bowl. Stir with the spoon until combined. Use the rubber scraper to fold in the whipped dessert topping.

2   Spoon dip into one serving bowl. Put granola in the other serving bowl. Use a fork to dip fruit in dip and then in granola. Makes 6 servings.

Nutrition Facts per serving: 136 calories, 3 g total fat, 0 mg cholesterol, 59 mg sodium, 26 g carbohydrate, 2 g fiber, 2 g protein.

✦🐚✦🐚✦🐚✦🐚✦🐚✦
Princess Party Tips
Set out a variety of different colored plastic dinglehoppers (forks) and let your guests choose which one to use.

Use a fork, or dinglehopper
as Scuttle would say, to dip
your fruit into this sweet dip
and then into the granola.

Beach Bags

Ingredients

1 package 100-calorie cinnamon-flavor bear-shape graham snack cookies

¼ cup vanilla or fruit-flavor low-fat yogurt

¼ cup fresh blueberries

Utensils
Kitchen scissors
Small spoon
Measuring cups

1 Use scissors to cut open bag of cookies along one of the short ends. Spoon yogurt over cookies in bag. Top with blueberries. Serve from the bag with a spoon. Makes 1 serving.

Nutrition Facts per serving: 225 calories, 4 g total fat, 6 mg cholesterol, 251 mg sodium, 41 g carbohydrate, 2 g fiber, 7 g protein.

Whether you're sunning your tail on the beach or just coming home from a long day at school, this quick-to-fix snack is sure to bring a smile to your face.

Sandy ❀ Scoops

Ingredients

2 7- to 8-inch flour tortillas

   Nonstick cooking spray

2 teaspoons sugar

¼ teaspoon ground cinnamon

4 4-ounce cups fruit-flavor or plain applesauce

Utensils

Cutting board
Pizza cutter or sharp knife
Large baking sheet
Measuring spoons
Small bowl
Small spoon
Hot pads
Wire cooling rack

1 Preheat the oven to 375°F. Place flour tortillas on cutting board. Use pizza cutter or sharp knife to cut each tortilla into eight wedges. Place tortilla wedges in a single layer on the ungreased baking sheet. Generously coat tortilla wedges with cooking spray. Stir together sugar and cinnamon in the small bowl. Evenly sprinkle sugar mixture over tortilla wedges.

2 Place baking sheet in oven. Bake for 7 to 9 minutes or until light brown. Turn off oven. Use hot pads to remove baking sheet from oven to cooling rack. Let cool completely.

3 Use the baked tortilla wedges to scoop up the applesauce. Makes 4 servings.

Nutrition Facts per serving: 136 calories, 1 g total fat, 0 mg cholesterol, 60 mg sodium, 30 g carbohydrate, 1 g fiber, 1 g protein.

The cinnamon-sugar topping on these tortilla scoops looks like sand, especially to a mermaid. Take them for a dip in a "sea" of applesauce for a swimmingly good snack.

Princess Party Tips

Serve fruit-flavor and plain applesauce so your friends can try each with their scoops.

Ocean Shimmers

Ingredients

1½ cups lemon-lime carbonated beverage

3 envelopes unflavored gelatin

1 6-ounce can frozen lemonade concentrate, thawed or ¾ cup orange juice

Colored sugar, edible glitter, or fresh fruit

Utensils

8x8x2-inch baking pan
Foil
Measuring cups
Medium saucepan
Wooden spoon
Hot pads
Cooling rack
Plastic wrap
Cutting board
1½-inch fish-shape or other cookie cutters or table knife

1 Line the bottom and sides of baking pan with the foil. Press the foil into the pan where the sides and bottom meet. Smooth out the foil with your fingers to remove wrinkles. Save until Step 3.

2 Pour the carbonated beverage into the saucepan. Sprinkle the gelatin over the beverage. Let stand for 1 minute. Put the pan on the stove burner. Turn the burner to high heat. Heat until mixture begins to boil, stirring all the time with the wooden spoon. Boil and stir until the gelatin is dissolved. Turn off burner. Use hot pads to remove saucepan from burner to cooling rack.

3 Pour the thawed concentrate into the pan with the gelatin mixture; stir well. Pour juice mixture into the foil-lined pan. Cover pan with plastic wrap and refrigerate about 4 hours or until firm.

4 Turn the pan upside down on the cutting board to remove the gelatin. Use cookie cutters or a table knife to cut the gelatin into shapes. Sprinkle with colored sugar or decorate with fresh fruit. Makes 36 pieces.

Nutrition Facts per piece: 39 calories, 0 g total fat, 0 mg cholesterol, 35 mg sodium, 10 g carbohydrate, 0 g fiber, 1 g protein.

Just like coral shimmers on the reef,
these wiggly gelatin snacks really sparkle
when the sun shines off them.

Salt-free Floats

Ingredients

1½ cups orange or pineapple juice, chilled

1½ cups carbonated water, chilled

1 cup mango, peach, or strawberry sorbet

Orange wedges (optional)

Mango slices (optional)

Utensils

Measuring cups

Large pitcher

Large spoon

Ice cream scoop or large spoon

4 6- to 8-ounce glasses

1 Put orange juice and carbonated water in the pitcher; stir to combine. Place a scoop of sorbet in each of four 6- to 8-ounce glasses. Fill each glass with carbonated fruit juice. If you like, garnish with orange wedges and mango slices. Makes 4 servings.

Nutrition Facts per serving: 102 calories, 0 g total fat, 0 mg cholesterol 25 mg sodium, 28 g carbohydrate, 0 g fiber, 1 g protein.

★❀★❀★❀★❀★❀★
Princess Party Tips

Ask each guest to bring a special glass to the party and then fill each glass with these floats.

Drinking salt water all day gets a little old so here's one of Flounder's recipes for a fruity drink that will also keep you cool on a hot, sunny day.

Dinner Is Served

Meals are quite formal in the Beast's castle, especially the evening meal. There are lots of dishes and everyone must dress up in their finest attire.

Are you ready for a meal fit for the Beast? As the castle staff would say, "Be our guest!"

Castle Calzones

Ingredients

Nonstick cooking spray

1¼ cups chopped sliced cooked ham

½ cup frozen baby peas, thawed

¾ cup shredded cheddar cheese

1 13.8-ounce package refrigerated pizza dough

1 tablespoon low-fat milk

Pizza sauce (optional)

Utensils

Large baking sheet
Foil
Measuring cups
Medium bowl
Wooden spoon
Rolling pin (optional)
Pizza cutter
Large spoon
Pastry brush
Fork
Hot pads
Wire cooling rack
Wide metal spatula

1 Preheat the oven to 400°F. Line the baking sheet with foil. Lightly coat the foil with nonstick cooking spray. Save until Step 2. For filling, put ham, peas, and cheese into the bowl; stir with the wooden spoon to combine. Save until Step 2.

2 Unroll the pizza dough on a lightly floured surface. Roll or press dough into a 12-inch square. Using the pizza cutter or a sharp knife, cut into nine 4-inch squares. Spoon about ⅓ cup filling into the middle of each of the squares. Use the pastry brush or fingers to moisten the edges of the dough with water. Fold the dough over the filling. Use the tines of the fork to seal the dough. Use the fork to prick holes in the top of each calzone to allow steam to escape. Place calzones on the prepared baking sheet. Use the pastry brush to brush the top of each calzone with milk.

3 Put the baking sheet in the oven. Bake for 13 to 15 minutes or until golden. Turn off oven. Use the hot pads to remove baking sheet from the oven. Put baking sheet on the wire rack. Cool calzones on the baking sheet for 10 minutes. Use the wide metal spatula to remove the calzones from the baking sheet. If you like, serve warm with pizza sauce. Makes 9 calzones.

Nutrition Facts per calzone: 166 calories, 7 g total fat, 21 mg cholesterol, 452 mg sodium, 18 g carbohydrate, 1 g fiber, 8 g protein.

A calzone is like a sandwich that is sealed on all sides, like the Beast's castle, which is closed to outsiders. But unlike the castle, you don't need permission to get inside these hot sandwiches—just pick one up and take a bite.

Won't You Be Mine? Pizza

Ingredients

Nonstick cooking spray

12 thin slices mozzarella cheese

1 13.8-ounce package refrigerated pizza dough

1 8-ounce can pizza sauce

½ cup sliced Canadian-style bacon (2 ounces)

2 tablespoons grated Parmesan cheese

Utensils

Large baking sheet
2½- to 3-inch heart-shaped cookie cutter
Ruler
Table knife
Measuring cups
Measuring spoons
Hot pads
Wire cooling rack
Pizza cutter

1 Preheat the oven to 400°F. Lightly coat the baking sheet with cooking spray. Using the heart-shape cutter, cut heart shapes from cheese slices. Set aside cutouts until Step 3. (Save scraps for another use.)

2 Unroll the pizza dough on the prepared baking sheet. Use fingers to press dough to a 16x12-inch rectangle. Use the table knife to spread pizza sauce over pizza dough. Arrange Canadian-style bacon over sauce. Sprinkle with Parmesan cheese.

3 Place baking sheet in oven. Bake for 10 minutes. Use hot pads to remove baking sheet from oven and place on cooling rack. Arrange cheese cutouts over the top of the pizza. Use hot pads to return baking sheet to oven. Bake 2 to 3 minutes more or until cheese is melted and crust is golden. Turn off oven. Use hot pads to remove baking sheet from oven to cooling rack. Cool on wire rack for 5 minutes. Use pizza cutter or a sharp knife to cut into 12 squares. Makes 12 pizza squares.

Nutrition Facts per square: 175 calories, 12 g total fat, 21 mg cholesterol, 519 mg sodium, 18 g carbohydrate, 1 g fiber, 11 g protein.

Princess Party Tips

This pizza is perfect for a Valentine's Day party. Serve it on red plates or use red construction paper to cut out heart-shaped placemats.

The Beast really likes Belle, but he has a hard time showing it. This heart-topped pizza should do the trick. Make it to show someone special how much they mean to you.

Hothead Skillet

Ingredients

8   ounces lean ground beef

1   8-ounce can tomato sauce

1   15-ounce can tomato puree

1   cup dried multigrain elbow macaroni

½   cup finely chopped green sweet pepper

¼   cup water

1   tablespoon chili powder

½   cup shredded reduced-fat cheddar cheese

Utensils

Large skillet with lid
Wooden spoon
Colander
Medium bowl
Hot pads
Wire cooling rack
Disposable container
Measuring cups
Measuring spoons
Wire cooling rack

1 Put ground beef in a large skillet. Break up meat with wooden spoon. Put the skillet on a stove burner. Turn burner to medium-high heat.* Cook until the meat is no longer pink, stirring occassionally with the wooden spoon. This will take 8 to 10 minutes. Turn off burner. Place the colander over the medium bowl. Use hot pads to remove skillet from the burner. Place skillet on the cooling rack. Spoon meat and juices into the colander and let the fat drain into the bowl. Spoon meat back into skillet. Put cooled fat in a container and throw it away.

2 Stir tomato sauce, tomato puree, uncooked macaroni, sweet pepper, water, and chili powder into skillet with meat. Put skillet on burner. Turn burner to medium-high heat. Bring tomato sauce mixture to a boil. Turn down heat to medium-low. Cover skillet with lid. Cook about 20 minutes or until macaroni is tender, stirring often.

3 Use hot pads to remove skillet from burner. Place on cooling rack; sprinkle with cheddar cheese. Cover with lid and let stand about 2 minutes or until the cheese is melted. Makes 4 servings.

Nutrition Facts per serving: 295 calories, 9 g total fat, 45 mg cholesterol, 884 mg sodium, 35 g carbohydrate, 6 g fiber, 22 g protein.

*Note: Ask an adult to help you cook the meat and drain the hot grease from the pan.

Gaston has a hot temper, especially when he encounters the Beast. This chili-seasoned dinner isn't quite as spicy hot, but it will sure wake up your taste buds.

Beastly Good Burgers

Ingredients

1 pound lean ground beef

2 tablespoons bottled barbecue sauce

2 tablespoons pineapple preserves

12 small whole wheat dinner rolls, split

¼ cup french-fried onions

Bottled barbecue sauce or ketchup

Utensils

15x10x1-inch baking pan

Foil

Large mixing bowl

Wooden spoon

Measuring spoons

Ruler

Instant-read thermometer

Hot pads

Serving plate

Wide metal spatula

Measuring cups

1 Preheat the oven to 400°F. Line baking pan with foil. Put ground beef in bowl. Break up meat with a wooden spoon. Add 2 tablespoons barbecue sauce and pineapple preserves to meat. Stir well to combine. Use your hands to divide meat mixture into 12 equal portions. Shape each portion into a flat, round patty that measures about 2 inches across. Place patties on baking pan.

2 Put pan in oven. Bake for 15 minutes or until no pink remains and the centers reach 160°F. Ask an adult to help you check the temperature with an instant-read thermometer. Turn off oven. Use hot pads to remove baking pan from oven.

3 Place bottom halves of the dinner rolls on a serving plate. Use the wide metal spatula to lift burgers from baking pan and set them on the roll bottoms. Sprinkle burgers evenly with French-fried onions. If you like, top with additional barbecue sauce or ketchup. Cover with roll tops. Makes 12 mini burgers.

Nutrition Facts per burger: 163 calories, 6 g total fat, 25 mg cholesterol, 201 mg sodium, 18 g carbohydrate, 2 g fiber, 10 g protein.

Princess Party Tips

These are mini burgers, so why not host a party with other mini foods? Set out baby carrots for a side dish and animal crackers for dessert.

These mini burgers are made extra special with barbecue sauce and pineapple preserves. The Beast can eat 10 of them, but one is enough for Belle. (She likes to save room for dessert!)

Set the Mood Ravioli

Ingredients

1   9-ounce package refrigerated whole wheat four cheese ravioli

1   medium zucchini and/or yellow summer squash, halved lengthwise and cut into ½-inch thick slices

1   cup purchased pasta sauce

1   cup canned cannellini beans (white kidney beans) rinsed and drained

2   tablespoons finely shredded or grated Parmesan cheese

Utensils

Large saucepan
Colander
Hot pads
Measuring cups
Wooden spoon
Wire cooling rack
Measuring spoons

1 Cook ravioli in the large saucepan following the ravioli package directions. Add the zucchini slices to the pasta the last 3 minutes of cooking. Turn off the burner. Place colander in sink. Use hot pads to remove saucepan from burner. Carefully pour ravioli mixture into the colander to drain.

2 Add the pasta sauce and beans to the empty saucepan. Stir with wooden spoon until mixed. Put the saucepan on a stove burner. Turn burner to medium heat. Bring mixture to a boil. Add drained pasta mixture and heat through, stirring frequently with the wooden spoon. Turn off burner. Use hot pads to remove saucepan from burner to a cooling rack. To serve, sprinkle each serving with Parmesan cheese. Makes 4 servings.

Nutrition Facts per serving: 288 calories, 8 g total fat, 44 mg cholesterol, 838 mg sodium, 41 g carbohydrate, 8 g fiber, 16 g protein.

Lumiere uses candlelight to set a relaxing mood at dinner. Serve a delicious meal and you have an evening to remember. Make this pasta recipe for your family and have Mom light a candle. Then pretend you're dining in the castle!

Not French (Fried) Chicken

Ingredients

½ cup low-fat mayonnaise

4 teaspoons Dijon-style mustard

1 tablespoon honey

¼ cup all-purpose flour

⅛ teaspoon salt

1 pound skinless, boneless chicken breast halves, cut into 1½-inch pieces

1 egg, lightly beaten

2 tablespoons low-fat milk

30 whole wheat or regular round crackers, finely crushed (1¼ cups)

Utensils

3 small bowls
Spoon
Measuring cups
Measuring spoons
Plastic wrap
Large plastic bag
Baking sheet
Hot pads
Wire cooling rack
Waxed paper, if warming sauce

1 Preheat the oven to 425°F.

2 For honey-mustard dip, in a small bowl use a spoon to stir together mayonnaise, mustard, and honey. Cover with plastic wrap and refrigerate until serving time.

3 In the plastic bag combine flour and salt. Add chicken pieces, a few at a time, to the flour mixture. Close the bag; shake to coat chicken pieces. Set aside chicken for later in Step 4.

4 In a small bowl stir together egg and milk. Place crushed crackers in another small bowl. Dip coated chicken pieces, a few at a time, into the egg mixture. Roll the pieces in crackers. Place in a single layer on a large ungreased baking sheet.

5 Put baking sheet in the oven. Bake for 10 to 12 minutes or until chicken is no longer pink. Turn off oven. Use hot pads to remove baking sheet from the oven to cooling rack.

6 Serve with cold or warm honey-mustard dip. To warm dip, cover with waxed paper and microwave on 100% power (high) for 30 seconds or until heated through. Makes 4 servings.

Nutrition Facts per serving: 401 calories, 17 g total fat, 129 mg cholesterol, 691 mg sodium, 28 g carbohydrate, 1 g fiber, 31 g protein.

Princess Party Tips

Set out pretty dishes filled with other dipping sauces, such as barbecue sauce or light Ranch dressing, as well as the honey-mustard dip.

Living in France doesn't mean you have to french-fry everything. These chicken strips look and taste fried but are really baked in the oven.

Mini Meatball Buns

Ingredients

18 ½-ounce frozen cooked Italian meatballs, thawed

1 cup marinara or pasta sauce

6 whole wheat cocktail buns, split and toasted, if you like

1 cup shredded reduced-fat mozzarella cheese

Sweet red pepper strips (optional)

Utensils

Measuring cups
Large saucepan
Wooden spoon
Hot pads
Wire cooling rack

1 Put the meatballs and pasta sauce in the saucepan. Put saucepan on burner. Turn burner to medium heat. Cook meatballs, stirring occasionally with the wooden spoon, until meatballs are heated through. Turn off burner. Use hot pads to remove saucepan from burner to cooling rack.

2 To serve, place three meatballs with some of the sauce on the bottom half of each bun. Sprinkle with some of the cheese. Add bun tops. If desired, serve with sweet red pepper strips. Makes 6 servings.

Nutrition Facts per serving: 294 calories, 16 g total fat, 45 mg cholesterol, 737 mg sodium, 23 g carbohydrate, 4 g fiber, 14 g protein.

The French are known for their cooking, so why not give it a try at home? These hot beef sandwiches are served with a dipping sauce that the French call "au jus." As Lumiere would say, "*C'est magnifique!*"

Happily Ever After Treats

When Sleeping Beauty awoke from her long nap, she married her prince and her days became sweeter than ever before. Add a little sweetness to your days with these royal treats.

Dreamy Fruit Cobbler

Ingredients

3 cups frozen fruit, such as sliced peaches, raspberries, and/or blueberries, thawed

2 tablespoons sugar

1 tablespoon quick-cooking tapioca

1 cup packaged reduced-fat biscuit mix

1 tablespoon sugar

¼ cup low-fat milk

Cinnamon-sugar (optional)

Utensils

Measuring cups
Measuring spoons
Medium mixing bowl
Wooden spoon
4 5- to 6-ounce custard cups or baking dishes
Small mixing bowl
Large spoon
Shallow baking pan
Hot pads
Wire cooling rack

1 Preheat the oven to 400°F. Put the fruit, 2 tablespoons sugar, and the tapioca into the medium bowl. Use the wooden spoon to stir the fruit mixture until well combined. Evenly divide the fruit mixture between the custard cups. Save for Step 2.

2 Put the biscuit mix, 1 tablespoon sugar, and the milk in the small bowl. Use the large spoon and stir until combined. Evenly spoon the batter over the fruit mixture. If you like, sprinkle tops lightly with cinnamon-sugar. Place the custard cups in the shallow baking pan.

3 Place the baking pan in the oven. Bake about 25 minutes or until filling is bubbly and topping is golden. Turn off oven. Use the hot pads to remove baking pan from oven. Let cool about 30 minutes on the cooling rack. Serve warm. Makes 4 servings.

Nutrition Facts per serving: 210 calories, 5 g total fat, 0 mg cholesterol, 377 mg sodium, 41 g carbohydrate. 2 g fiber, 4 g protein.

Once upon a dream, Princess Aurora met her prince. But after meeting him in the forest, will she ever see him again? While you await the answer, enjoy this dreamy fruit cobbler, topped with a warm, flaky biscuit.

Awaken the Kingdom Pudding

Ingredients

2 eggs, lightly beaten

2 cups lowfat milk

3 tablespoons packed brown sugar

1 teaspoon vanilla

½ teaspoon pumpkin pie spice or ground cinnamon

5 cups dry oatmeal bread cubes*

2 medium bananas, halved lengthwise and sliced

½ cup chopped walnuts or pecans, toasted (optional)

Utensils

Measuring cups
Measuring spoons
Medium mixing bowl
Wire whisk
8x8x2-inch baking dish
Wooden spoon
Table knife
Hot pads
Wire cooling rack

1 Preheat the oven to 350°F. Put eggs, milk, brown sugar, vanilla, and pumpkin pie spice in the medium bowl. Use wire whisk to combine all ingredients. Put the bread cubes, bananas, and walnuts, if desired, in the baking dish. Use a wooden spoon to evenly spread mixture into the dish. Evenly pour the egg mixture over the bread mixture in the dish. Stir until all bread is moistened.

2 Put dish in oven. Bake for 35 to 40 minutes or until a table knife inserted near the center comes out clean. Turn off oven. Use hot pads to remove dish from oven. Place dish on a wire rack to cool slightly before serving. Serve warm. Makes 9 servings.

Nutrition Facts per serving: 162 calories, 3 g total fat, 50 mg cholesterol, 221 mg sodium, 28 g carbohydrate, 2 g fiber, 6 g protein.

*Note: For 5 cups dry bread cubes, turn on oven to 350°F. Spread 8½ cups bread cubes (11 slices) in a shallow baking pan. Bake for 10 to 15 minutes or until bread cubes are dry, stirring twice; cool on a wire rack.

Princess Party Tips

Make this with your friends on the night of a sleepover and your guests can have it for breakfast the next morning. Serve with fresh banana slices and orange juice.

When the kingdom finally wakes from slumber, the people will be awfully hungry. This bread pudding is just what they need. With bananas and bread, it can serve as breakfast after a long sleep or be eaten as dessert after a meal.

Little 👑 Jewels

Ingredients

- 1   large banana,
  2 kiwifruit, and/or
  1 cup strawberries
- 1   8-ounce package light
  cream cheese
- ¼   cup strawberry, peach,
  pineapple, or other
  preserves
- 1   2.1-ounce package (15)
  miniature phyllo dough
  shells
- 2   tablespoons chocolate
  ice cream topping
  (optional)

Utensils
Cutting board
Sharp knife
Measuring cups
Small mixing bowl
Wooden spoon
Small spoon
Measuring spoons

1 If using the banana, remove the peel and throw away. Place the banana on the cutting board. Use the knife to cut the banana into small pieces. If using the kiwifruits, have an adult remove the peel. Place the kiwifruit on the cutting board. Use the knife to cut into small pieces. If using the strawberries, place them on the cutting board. Use the knife to cut off the green tops. Throw the green tops away. Cut the strawberries into small pieces. Save the fruit until Step 3.

2 Put cream cheese and preserves in the small bowl. Use the wooden spoon to combine. Use the small spoon to spoon some of the cream cheese mixture into each phyllo shell.

3 Divide the fruit among the shells. If desired, drizzle some of the ice cream topping over fruit. Serve immediately or refrigerate. Makes 15 tarts.

Nutrition Facts per tart: 76 calories, 3 g total fat,
7 mg cholesterol, 83 mg sodium, 10 g carbohydrate,
0 g fiber, 2 g protein.

Royalty always has jewels in all kinds of sparkling colors. Pretend these little tarts are jewels by using different-colored fruits in each one: strawberries for rubies, blueberries for blue sapphires and kiwifruit for jade jewels.

The Fairies' Favorite Cake

Ingredients

4   ounces purchased angel food cake

½   of an 8-ounce package reduced-fat cream cheese, softened

2   tablespoons strawberry preserves

2   tablespoons low-fat milk

3   cups fresh raspberries, blackberries, and/or blueberries

Utensils

Cutting board
Serrated knife
Measuring cups
15x10x1-inch baking pan
Hot pads
Wire cooling rack
Wooden spoon
Medium mixing bowl
Electric mixer
Measuring spoons
Rubber scraper
6 dessert dishes
Large spoon

1   Preheat the oven to 300°F. Put the cake on the cutting board. Have an adult use the serrated knife to cut the cake into cubes (you should have about 4 cups of cake cubes). Put cake cubes in the baking pan. Put the baking pan in the oven. Bake for 20 minutes. Turn off oven. Use the hot pads to remove the pan from the oven. Put pan on the wire rack. Stir 2 times with a wooden spoon. Let the cake cubes cool in the pan for 15 minutes.

2   Meanwhile, put cream cheese in the medium bowl. Beat with the electric mixer on medium speed for 30 seconds. Gradually beat in preserves and milk until smooth, occasionally stopping the mixer and scraping the side of the bowl with the rubber scraper.

3   Divide cake cubes among the 6 dessert dishes. Top with fruit. Spoon cream cheese mixture over fruit and cake cubes. Makes 6 servings.

Nutrition Facts per serving: 151 calories, 5 g total fat, 15 mg cholesterol, 222 mg sodium, 24 g carbohydrate, 4 g fiber, 4 g protein.

Princess Party Tips

Put together this dessert in clear, plastic cups so your guests can see all the pretty layers.

When Fauna makes Aurora a birthday cake, she finds it's a little harder than she thought. This cake is much easier. Just bake the cake and top with fruit.

Hail to the King Stacks

Ingredients

4 frozen multigrain waffles

2 3.5-ounce (single-serving) containers lemon or vanilla pudding

1 cup fresh blueberries

Utensils

Electric toaster
Cutting board
Sharp knife
4 serving plates
Measuring spoons
Small spoon
Measuring cups

1 Toast waffles as directed on package. Place toasted waffles on cutting board. Cut each waffle in half with the knife. Place one waffle half on each plate. Remove and set aside 2 tablespoons of the pudding. Divide the remaining pudding evenly among the waffle halves on plates. Top pudding with some of the blueberries. Top with remaining waffle halves. Evenly spoon the reserved 2 tablespoons pudding on top of the waffles and decorate each stack with remaining blueberries. Makes 4 servings.

Nutrition Facts per serving: 154 calories, 3 g total fat, 0 mg cholesterol, 285 mg sodium, 32 g carbohydrate, 2 g fiber, 3 g protein.

This dessert is easy to make but looks like something fit for a king. If you don't have blueberries, try fresh strawberries.

Change the Dress Color
Biscuits

Ingredients

1   10- to 12-ounce package (10 total) refrigerated biscuits

10   teaspoons creamy peanut butter

10   ½-inch chunks fresh apple

2½   teaspoons pink and/or blue decorating sugar

Utensils

Table knife
Measuring spoons
Large cookie sheet
Hot pads
Wire cooling rack
Wide metal spatula

1   Preheat the oven to 350°F. Use the palm of your hand to flatten each biscuit. Using the table knife, spread 1 teaspoon peanut butter in the center of each biscuit. Place an apple chunk on top of the peanut butter. Use your fingers to bring the edges of the biscuit up and around the apple to enclose; pinch the dough well to seal it shut. Place biscuits on the ungreased cookie sheet. Sprinkle each biscuit with ¼ teaspoon of the colored sugar.

2   Place the cookie sheet in the oven. Bake about 15 minutes or until the biscuit bottoms are golden brown. Turn off the oven. Use the hot pads to remove the cookie sheet from the oven to a cooling rack. Use the wide metal spatula to remove the biscuits from the cookie sheet. Serve the biscuits warm. Makes 10 biscuits.

Nutrition Facts per biscuit: 142 calories, 7 g total fat, 0 mg cholesterol, 331 mg sodium, 17 g carbohydrate, 1 g fiber, 4 g protein.

What color should Aurora's birthday dress be? The fairies can't decide, so vote for your favorite by decorating these sweet biscuits in colored sugar.

Pretty as a
Princess Parfait

Ingredients

1   8-ounce package light cream cheese, softened

1   tablespoon low-fat milk

1   teaspoon vanilla

1   cup coarsely crushed pretzels

1½ cups sliced fresh strawberries

4   whole pretzels (optional)

Utensils

Measuring spoons
Small bowl
Wooden spoon
Measuring cups
Four 8-ounce parfait or drinking glasses
Small spoon
Plastic wrap (if chilling)

1 Put cream cheese, milk, and vanilla in the small bowl. Stir with the wooden spoon until smooth. Divide half of the crushed pretzels among the glasses. Spoon half of the cream cheese mixture over pretzels. Layer half of the strawberries over cream cheese mixture. Repeat layers. Serve immediately, or cover with plastic wrap and refrigerate for up to 4 hours before serving. If you like, top each serving with a whole pretzel. Makes 4 servings.

Nutrition Facts per serving: 188 calories, 9 g total fat, 27 mg cholesterol, 484 mg sodium, 21 g carbohydrate, 2 g fiber, 8 g protein.

Princess Party Tips
If you don't have parfait glasses, you can use any tall glasses. Or ask your mom to buy some tall plastic glasses in pastel colors to serve these in. Then each guest can take one home.

Serve these at your next princess party and your guests will love how they look as much as how they taste! Pretty pink strawberries are used here, but you could substitute raspberries, blueberries, or most any fruit.

True Love's Kiss Cups

Ingredients

1   4-serving-size package instant chocolate pudding mix

2   cups low-fat milk

¼   of an 8-ounce container frozen light or regular whipped dessert topping, thawed

⅛   to ¼ teaspoon mint extract

1   or 2 drops red food coloring

1   cup fresh raspberries, blueberries, or chopped strawberries

Frozen light or regular whipped dessert topping, thawed

Utensils

Measuring cups
Measuring spoons
Small mixing bowl
Large spoon
6 dessert bowls
Plastic wrap

1   Prepare pudding mix according to package directions using the 2 cups low-fat milk. Set aside until Step 2. Put dessert topping and mint extract in the small bowl. Use the spoon to gently stir until combined. Add food coloring to make the color you like.

2   Layer half of the pudding among the 6 dessert bowls. Top with dessert topping, fruit, and remaining pudding. Cover bowls with plastic wrap and refrigerate for 2 hours or until set. If you like, top with additional whipped topping. Makes 6 servings.

Nutrition Facts per serving: 100 calories, 3 g total fat, 4 mg cholesterol, 256 mg sodium, 15 g carbohydrate, 2 g fiber, 4 g protein.

Princess Party Tips

Host a Sleeping Beauty party! Watch the movie with your friends and when Aurora is kissed by the prince, have these cups ready to serve.

Celebrate the awakening of Sleeping Beauty with these minty pudding cups. You can use any color for the whipped topping, but princess pink is used here.

Princess Party Planner

Hi! I'm Jasmine and I'm here to help you plan a party for you and your friends. It's as easy as making a wish! Just fill in the blanks and you're on your way to hosting a dreamy princess party.

My favorite color: _____

My favorite princess: _____

My favorite foods: _____
_____

My friends and I like to play
these games: _____
_____

My friends and I like this type of music:
_____

Recipes I want to make in this book for
my party: _____
_____

Friends I want to invite to my party:
_____
_____

Wasn't that easy? Now go over your party planner with an adult, and together you can plan your party.